SURVIVING
Social Media

3,154 likes

Shut Down the Haters

by Eric Braun

Consultant:
Matthew Meyers, MA, LMFT

COMPASS POINT BOOKS
a capstone imprint

is published by Compass Point Books, an imprint of Capstone.

710 Roe Crest Drive
North Mankato, Minnesota 56003
www.capstonepub.com

Library of Congress Cataloging-in-Publication Data is available on the Library of Congress website.

ISBN: 978-0-7565-6620-3 (hardcover)
ISBN: 978-0-7565-6664-7 (paperback)
ISBN: 978-0-7565-6628-9 (ebook PDF)

Summary: Nearly 75 percent of the U.S. population use social media. For students, it is often considered a lifeline to connecting with their peers and staying relevant. But there's a dark side as well. How much social media use is healthy? What happens when trolls take over? Where do you go for help? Readers will learn to understand the pros and cons of social media and how to make smart decisions about managing their online presence.

Image Credits
AP Photo: 18; Getty Images: Dustin Finkelstein, 14, Mike Coppola, 40; Newscom: agefotostock/Jim West, 32, CQ Roll Call/Tom Williams, 4 (bottom); North Wind Picture Archives: 16; Shutterstock: Ammit Jack, 53, Andrew Cline, 28, Antonio Guillem, 51, bibiphoto, 39, BigTunaOnline, 24, Brocreative, 7, carballo, 23 (top), chrisdorney, 19, 44, COMEO/Frederic Legrand, 21, Everett Collection, 17, fizkes, 12, Fleur_de_papier, 4 (top), 15, 26, 37 (top), 46, 58, GlebSStock, 41, Hadrian, 30, hafakot, 27, Hayk_Shalunts, 29, Jakraphong Photography, 20, Jarretera, 6, Jeff Pinette, 5, Julia Tim, 63, karelnoppe, 49, Kim Kelley-Wagner, 11, Kostsov, cover, Look Studio, 35, Odua Images, 54, pathdoc, 42, Pushkin, 37, Rawpixel.com, 10, 34, rvlsoft, 48, SeventyFour, 47, Tom Eversley, 9, Twin Design, 33, Zyabich, 23 (bottom)

Editorial Credits
Designer: Kay Fraser; Media Researcher: Eric Gohl; Production Specialist: Kathy McColley

Consultant Credit
Matthew Meyers, MA, LMFT

Printed in the United States. 5584

TABLE OF CONTENTS

CHAPTER 1

A CONNECTED WORLD

On February 14, 2018, students at Marjory Stoneman Douglas High School in Parkland, Florida, had their lives turned upside down. That was the day a former student took a semi-automatic rifle into the school and murdered 17 people, injuring 17 others. In the aftermath of the tragedy, a group of students who survived the shooting became powerful activists in the fight for stronger gun laws. They met with politicians and were interviewed on television. They held rallies and made speeches. But perhaps their most powerful tool was social media, where they used the hashtag #NeverAgain to spread their message. Their

School shooting survivor and activist David Hogg

tweets went viral. Their Never Again Facebook page quickly gained tens of thousands of followers. During the next two years, they influenced changes to laws all over the country and inspired countless people to vote for politicians who sided with their view.

FACT
125 million hashtags were shared every day on Twitter in 2018. Users posted about 500 million tweets per day.

A social media phenomenon doesn't have to be connected to a worldwide political movement for it to be powerful and important. In May 2019, a mother was walking with her 8-year-old daughter in Fort Worth, Texas, when something terrifying happened. A car suddenly pulled up, and a man got out and grabbed the little girl. He pulled her into the car and fought off the mom as she tried to rescue her daughter. Then he sped away. In an instant, the girl was gone.

Police launched a hunt right away. They issued an AMBER alert and canvassed the area. They also posted to social media a photo of the kidnapper and his car, taken from a Ring doorbell camera near the site. It quickly spread. Within hours, someone who had seen the photo online recognized the car at a motel in a nearby suburb.

They called the police, who rescued the girl and arrested the kidnapper. The girl was soon home safe with her family.

It was a scary story that could have had a much worse ending if not for social media. A Fort Worth police officer said afterward, "We do want to thank all of our followers. We're a good police department, we work hard, but with you on our side we're able to be more effective."

As of February 2020, nearly 1,000 children had been rescued because of AMBER Alerts.

The Bad with the Good

Social media has become a major part of our lives, and it goes way beyond spreading influence or capturing criminals. It's easy to use social media to hurt one another. Do any of these stories sound familiar?

A high-school sophomore finds herself the subject of rumors on social media and doesn't know how to defend herself. The built-in audience of social media makes it feel like everyone is laughing at her, and she's powerless to do anything.

A middle-school boy is harassed relentlessly for being gay. Because of social media, the bullying isn't confined to school—it follows him on his phone everywhere he goes.

Another boy is targeted and threatened for having the "wrong" friends. He doesn't feel safe, even at home, where violent messages continue to follow him.

A sixth grader is bullied so mercilessly on Snapchat and Facebook that she tries to take her own life three times. She goes into treatment for seven months but returns to find that the cyberbullying got worse while she was away. She changes schools four times looking for a fresh start, but the mistreatment follows her.

Cyberbullying affects everyone—the person being bullied, the person bullying, and the bystanders.

Heroes and Villains

Online, it's easy to imagine that our words are harmless when we hit Post, but often the stakes can become sky-high. Back in December 2013, in the early days of Twitter, a woman named Justine Sacco was traveling to South Africa to visit family. Before getting on a plane for her final connection, she tweeted a poorly worded joke to her 170 followers: "Going to Africa. Hope I don't get AIDS. Just kidding. I'm white!"

As Sacco later explained, she didn't really think that white people are immune to AIDS. "Only an *insane* person would think that white people don't get AIDS," she said. She was making a joke about people's ignorance, saying that people in the United States often aren't aware of what goes on in the rest of the world. Unfortunately for Sacco, in the world of social media, our words stand alone—we don't get to explain ourselves if they don't come off well.

And Sacco's words did not come off well. While she was on the 11-hour flight to South Africa with her phone turned off, her tweet was retweeted. And retweeted. And retweeted some more.

By the time she landed and turned on her phone, Sacco was the world's highest trending topic on Twitter. Thousands of people were insulting her, calling her racist—and worse. Her employers had seen the tweet and were preparing to fire her. Strangers were excitedly tracking her flight, waiting for her to land and discover that her life was ruined. The hashtag #HasJustineLandedYet spread like wildfire. Someone even showed up at the airport to take her photo as she got off the plane.

On the ground again, as Sacco's phone blew up, she quickly realized that nothing would ever be the same. She had to cut her vacation short because she and her family were threatened. She lost her job. She was recognized everywhere she went. She had been thoroughly shamed, and her name had become

The average adult checks their phone 58 times per day.

identified with racism and ignorance. Her life was in tatters.

Did Sacco deserve what she got? When it comes to social media, people tend to look at things in black and white with no room for gray. Writing about Sacco's situation, the journalist Jon Ronson said, " . . . with social media, we've created a stage for constant artificial high drama. Every day a new person emerges as a magnificent hero or a sickening villain." Often, we cut down others online in order to make ourselves feel superior.

A Mixed Bag

Social media platforms such as Twitter, Instagram, Facebook, Snapchat, TikTok, and others make our lives better in many ways. They help us keep in touch with family and friends. Social media gives us the chance to expand our social circles and meet people who share our interests. And if there's a cause or campaign we're passionate about or want to learn more about, social media is an easy and effective way to get involved.

On the other hand, it's no secret that social media does cause problems, particularly for kids and teens. Young people are still forming their identities. Negative feedback on social media can influence how they feel about themselves. Young people also tend to be concrete rather than abstract thinkers, as the ability to think more critically develops as people mature. The "black and white" view of the world that concrete thinkers have is often reinforced by information on social media.

The average teen gets more than 7 hours a day of screen time not related to schoolwork.

Young social media users often are more sensitive to advertising influence. Advertisers spend billions of dollars per year targeting young people. Companies work to develop brand loyalty and a need to fit in with the "right"

News of rallies and protests are shared via social media by political groups and hate groups alike.

products. Much of this advertising is for unhealthy things such as sugary drinks and junk food.

Businesses gather personal data through apps, especially social media apps. We willingly provide personal information and expose ourselves to location tracking. We let companies track our web browsing habits and buying history so they can target us with more ads.

Inaccurate news and misleading videos and stories, all of which reach us easily through social media, fuel our anger and divide us. Hate groups are organizations that verbally or physically attack people based on ethnicity, religion, sexual orientation, or gender identity. These groups use social media to recruit new members, and it works. These groups are growing, and their messages of hate are slowly becoming more mainstream.

If you say something that others don't like, or you represent an identity others are against, you may be harassed. Many people are taunted and threatened through social media every day. The fact that the threats are online rather than IRL—in real life—doesn't make them less real or less scary. People often have their personal information, including their address and names of family members, hacked and shared online.

On any day, you can be exposed to inappropriate or even dangerous things as you scroll through your news feed. You might see adults fighting and bullying one another, including politicians using their position to spread angry or mean-spirited messages about their opponents. You might see extreme anger and cynicism. Because social media is poorly regulated, violence and pornography are always one click away, no matter how old you are. Online predators use fake identities as they try to scam, exploit, or hurt others.

FACT
A 2019 study by market research company GlobalWebIndex found that the average social media user spent 2 hours and 16 minutes each day on social media platforms. That was about one-third of the total internet time and one-seventh of the time the user spent awake.

Other drawbacks of social media are less obvious but no less important. Too much time spent online may lead to depression, negative self-esteem, loneliness, and feelings of isolation. Seeing others having what seems like a great time without us can lead to FOMO, or fear of missing out. We may feel worse about our own lives, which seem ordinary in comparison. When friends, celebrities, or influencers—people with large followings who are paid to promote products on social media—share their carefully selected, flattering images, we may feel worse about our own appearance. That can cause us to develop unhealthy body images.

Even if things mostly go well online, many of us aren't developing social skills or making real-life connections. Sometimes we feel more distant from our friends and families, even as we learn the smallest details about others' lives through social media. Many of us have fewer face-to-face interactions, which are important for maturing and developing a healthy self-esteem.

So how can we get the benefits of social media while protecting ourselves from the negatives?

Social Network Users Worldwide (2010–2021)

About 3 billion of the world's 7.8 billion people have at least one social media account.

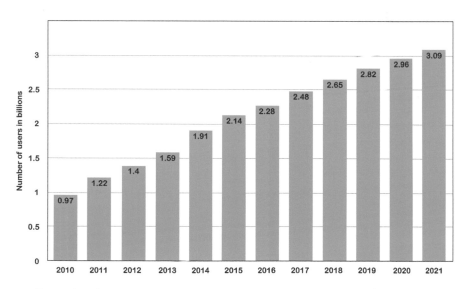

credit: statista https://www.statista.com/statistics/278414/number-of-worldwide-social-network-users/

SOCIAL MEDIA HELPS REUNITE TWINS

In February 2013, Anaïs Bordier was a 26-year-old French student studying fashion in London. One day she was watching a YouTube video and a face caught her attention—a face that looked amazingly like her own. A few weeks later, she noticed the same face again, this time in a trailer for the movie *21 & Over.*

Bordier was so struck by how much this other woman looked like her that she began to search online for information. She soon discovered that her look-alike was an American actress named Samantha Futerman. And she learned that Futerman, like herself, was born in South Korea and adopted as a baby. But what really shocked her was Futerman's birthday, November 19, 1987—the same day as her own!

Bordier began to think she might have discovered a twin she never knew. She messaged Futerman on Facebook, and the two started chatting. It turned out that both women were adopted from Busan, South Korea—Bordier by a French couple, Futerman by an American couple. Before long, the two were messaging and Skyping frequently. While Skyping one day, the two took DNA tests—tests that can tell if two people are related. They sent the results to a doctor who was an expert on twins, and they soon got confirmation of what they had suspected. They were indeed identical twins.

Eventually the twins met and became fast friends. In fact, they filmed most of their early social media and real-life exchanges. You can see their whole story in the 2015 documentary *Twinsters.*

CHAPTER 2

HISTORY OF SOCIAL MEDIA

People need each other. We always have.

Since the beginning of humankind, we've lived
in communities and relied on cooperation in order to
survive and thrive. There's safety in numbers. There's also
companionship. Getting along with others and managing
relationships isn't only necessary to survival, it's also key
to feeling happy and satisfied. Social interaction is a basic
human need. It's so important that isolated people often
suffer from anxiety, aggression, or hallucinations—even
decreased life expectancy.

When we're very young, our main social group is our
family. As we get older, we form social groups outside
the family. We look for people who share our interests.
For a 5-year-old, that might mean a shared love of toy
trucks or a cartoon character. As we get older, our interests
get broader and more complex. You might have a group of
friends who play the same sport as you, a group that likes
role-playing games, and a group you see only at school.

Prehistoric people told stories and shared news around the fire—the social media platform of ancient times.

Technology Brings Change

When the telegraph became commercially available in the mid-1800s, people were able to communicate instantly with people far away for the first time. By the end of that century and early the next century, the telephone and radio expanded our ability to socialize even more.

In the 1960s, people used networked computers to create early bulletin boards and chat rooms. At that time, computers were huge, expensive machines mostly used by the government and large corporations. In the late 1960s, the U.S. Department of Defense began work on a project called the Advanced Research Projects Agency Network (ARPANET). This network of computers was the forerunner of the internet. The first email was sent via ARPANET in

For the first time, the telegraph made long-distance communication possible by transmitting electrical signals over wires strung between stations.

1971. In the late 1970s, the first personal computers were available for use in people's homes.

Internet Relay Chat (IRC) was developed in 1988. This protocol allowed users to connect to computer servers and exchange text messages in real time, known as chatting. Chat groups soon connected people all over the world.

In 1989 scientist Tim Berners-Lee and his colleagues at the Swiss research laboratory CERN invented hypertext transfer protocol (HTTP). HTTP allowed the exchange of files between computer servers and browsers. The World Wide Web, or internet, was born.

By the early 1990s, companies including America Online (AOL) and Prodigy were on the internet with message forums that made online communication available to the average person. Personal computers became smaller and more affordable, and many households had them.

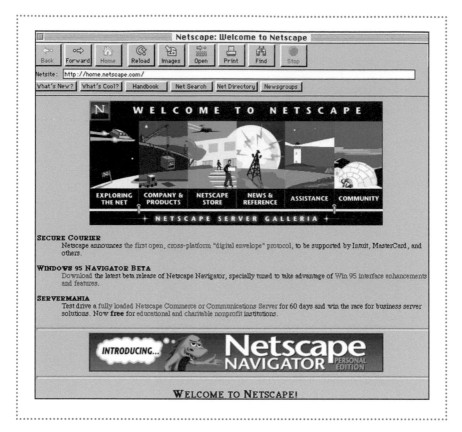

Homepage of Netscape Navigator, popular web browser of the 1990s

In the mid-1990s, sites allowing people to connect appeared on the internet. In 1995 came Classmates.com, a forerunner of what we consider social media today. This site, which still exists, allows people to find and connect with former classmates. In 1997 the MacroView company launched SixDegrees.com, which is generally considered to be the first modern-day social media site. It was the first to feature user profiles, a friends list, and school affiliation all on one platform. SixDegrees users could send messages to one another and post bulletin board messages. Blogging sites such as LiveJournal started popping up just before the end of the century.

Modern Era of Social Networking

Social media as you might recognize it today evolved shortly after that, with 2003 being a critical year. That year saw the rise of one of the first big platforms, Friendster, which was launched in 2002. It had many of the same features as SixDegrees but focused more on sharing media such as music. It also acted as a dating service. Also in 2003, LinkedIn hit the scene as a social-networking site for workers and job-seekers. It's still a popular platform today.

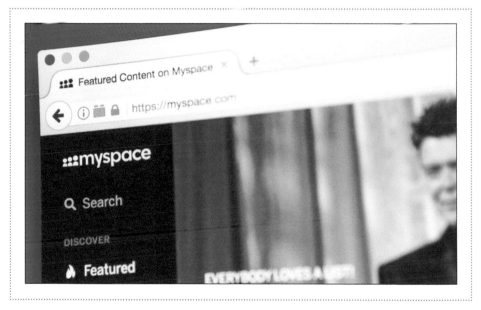

Homepage of the social networking site Myspace in April 2017

Myspace also launched in 2003. By 2005 it was the world's largest social media platform. Users could customize their profiles and embed music and videos on their pages, which was revolutionary at the time. By

August 2006, Myspace had 100 million users, and global media companies competed to buy it.

Sadly for Myspace, its position as the king of social media was brief. Facebook, which launched in 2004 as a resource for students at Harvard University in Massachusetts, expanded to the general public in 2006. It grew quickly due to its user-friendly interface and customizable profiles. By 2008 it had overtaken Myspace. Facebook introduced the Like button as a way for users to easily interact on the platform. User posts track the number of likes they gain.

FACT
In 2016 Facebook expanded the Like button into Reactions, which allows users to react with an icon that indicates Love, Haha, Wow, Sad, or Angry.

Other innovations adding to Facebook's appeal included its news feed. In this feature, a user can see other users' posts, profile changes, upcoming events, and more information. Facebook made adding photos easy, allowing users to add captions and tag friends. Instant messaging was also key to Facebook's popularity, allowing users to chat in groups or one on one. Messaging was later expanded into a separate app.

Facebook was also a pioneer in making money through advertising. A 2017 analysis determined that the company made a little more than $20 per user through ads. The data Facebook collects on its users also helps its advertisers target ads to certain audiences. By October 2012, Facebook had 1 billion active monthly users. In 2019 it had 2.4 billion users. In 2018 the company earned $55 billion in revenue.

Facebook founder Mark Zuckerberg's net worth is estimated at $57.3 billion.

YouTube launched in 2005, allowing users to create and share videos with their subscribers. The following year, Twitter came along. Twitter users posted 140-character messages—later increased to 280 characters—called tweets, which could be viewed by their followers. Rather than selecting who may follow them, as on other social media sites, Twitter users could follow anyone they wanted. This allowed people access to the posts of celebrities, athletes, politicians, and other public figures, which was unheard of earlier. Twitter continues to be one of the giants of social networking.

It's a Social Media World

By the end of the 2010s, social media was a virtually unavoidable part of life. Businesses created social media profiles and spent huge parts of their advertising budgets on social media. Reaching potential customers through social media was invaluable because customers provided so much information about themselves in their bios and posts. Businesses could target their ads and posts to specific users. They even used location check-ins and tracking, which social media platforms included in their apps, to sharpen their marketing.

Although other music-based social networks had been available for some time, Spotify began to take over that market when it was launched in 2008. This ushered in the era of music streaming, which greatly reduced sales of compact discs and vinyl albums.

Spotify reaches almost half of 16- to 24-year-olds in the United States each week.

When Instagram launched in 2010, it changed social networking again by putting even more focus on images. By making it easier than ever for users to create, edit, and share photos, its popularity skyrocketed and gave Facebook its stiffest competition. The age of selfies was born. The following year, Snapchat introduced the idea of disappearing messages and stories—posts that are deleted after they are viewed. More recently, TikTok bought Musical.ly in 2017 and became the biggest app used to shoot, edit, and share short videos.

FACT

The Oxford English Dictionary named selfie as its word of the year in 2013.

Today most social media platforms allow users to share words, music, photos, videos, or a combination of those. Some, including Instagram, Snapchat, and TikTok, are more popular with younger users. Others, such as Facebook, appeal to older audiences. Most people use more than one platform. With social media, people and businesses can reach a huge audience. It's difficult to imagine what life would be like without social media.

There are an estimated 500 million TikTok users around the world.

Timeline of Social Media

1968: The U.S. Department of Defense begins developing ARPANET

1971: First email is sent

1983: The word *internet* is first used

1988: IRC allows users to exchange text messages over the internet

1989: World Wide Web is invented

1995: Classmates.com launches

1997: SixDegrees.com launches

2002: Friendster launches

2003: LinkedIn and Myspace launch

2004: Harvard version of Facebook launches

2005: YouTube launches

2006: Twitter launches

2006: Facebook is open to the general public; Friendster grows to 100 million users

2008: Spotify launches

2009: Facebook introduces the Like button; Whatsapp launches

2010: Instagram launches; 970 million users are on social media

2011: Snapchat launches

2012: Facebook has 1 billion active monthly users

2013: Selfie is *The Oxford English Dictionary's* word of the year

2015: 2.14 billion users are on social media

2017: TikTok buys Musical.ly

2018: 2.65 billion users are on social media; Facebook earns $55 billion in revenue

2020: The COVID-19 virus forces much of the world to rely solely on internet communication for work, school, and socializing

CHAPTER 3

MAKING CONNECTIONS

Social media satisfies our basic human social needs by allowing us to share about ourselves, find new connections, and be part of a community. But its popularity and usefulness go far beyond those things.

Networking

Social networking—it's in the name. Social media does a great job of bringing us together. We can share photos with loved ones who are miles away, helping us keep our relationships current and strong. When our loved ones see photos of our family members, pets, and activities, they may feel like they're more of a part of our lives.

People often share selfies with friends and family to stay connected. One poll found that every third photo taken is a selfie.

School social media sites help teachers and students communicate, making learning, keeping track of due dates, and turning in assignments more convenient. If you have a question about homework, you can reach out online to a teacher or fellow student for help. It's easy to share readings, notes, worksheets, and projects.

Social media can also connect you with new friends. If you love an obscure artist whom none of your local friends care about, you can find like-minded fans online and geek out together. You can follow that artist's activities and sometimes even connect with him or her directly. If you happen to *be* an obscure artist, you can share your work and find your audience. Social media gives us the chance to be creative and put our ideas or creations out there for others to experience. Videos, art, writings, music—even jokes—are easy to share online.

2020 presidential candidate Joe Biden posed with supporters in New Hampshire.

Becoming Involved

Is there a cause you believe in strongly enough to get involved? Maybe you want to support a political candidate or a social movement working to make positive changes in your community. With social media, it's easy to research the topic, find volunteer opportunities, and spread your passion to others.

For teens who feel isolated or marginalized, social media is a terrific way to find a supportive community. For example, the It Gets Better Project began in 2010 as a social media campaign to support young LGBTQ+ people. Since then, more than 70,000 people have shared their stories, providing not only hope and encouragement but also visibility and community to people all over the world.

The #MeToo movement was started to help survivors of sexual violence and to bring awareness to the problem.

Social media has also been great for bringing attention to misbehavior by those in power and giving marginalized people a voice. For example, social media played a critical role in revealing sexual harassment of women by high-powered men such as the movie producer Harvey Weinstein. Many women chose to bravely tell their stories on social networks with the hashtag #MeToo.

SOCIAL NETWORKING TO HELP PEOPLE IN NEED

In summer 2013, 15 U.S. high-school students spent a month in Ghana, Africa, on a service trip. During that month, they volunteered at several places, including a hospital, a housing project, and a center for children with disabilities called the Physically Challenged Action

Foundation (PCAF). The center's founder and director is Barimah Antwi, known as Mr. Ark.

For three of the students, the time at Mr. Ark's center was life changing. As student Ariel Kim recalled, "I'll never forget the boys and girls with not much more than the clothes on their backs who also had the biggest smiles on their faces."

Kim and two friends, Ivan Boyers and Andrew Goodrum, started talking about what they could do to help the center. When they returned home, they decided to do whatever they could to raise money to help the foundation build classrooms and dorms for the residents. They kept their promise and have raised more than $70,000. The key to their success? Social media.

Boyers explained, "Regarding our message, we really desired a brand. Therefore, we started by establishing a logo and a website that includes all the vital information for which donors would be looking. Unfortunately, we were still unknown to most of the world. Social media filled this void. Through Facebook, we post photos updating viewers about progress in Ghana but also simply informing potential donors of opportunities to give. Facebook provided a platform through which we could direct people straight to the donation page of our website. And the 'share' button has been a huge help to our spread."

School and Work Life

Using social media, you can network and meet people who can help you with your education or profession. You can reach out to meet someone who can help you get a job or teach you a new skill. You can learn about a company where you'd like to work, and the company can learn about you as well.

It's not too early to start thinking about your professional future. Your digital footprint is the trace you leave on the internet. When someone searches for you online, they can find your social media accounts and all the things you've posted, unless you've made your page settings private. Future employers, colleges, scholarship committees, and even clubs and social groups can use your digital footprint to decide whether you're a good fit for their organization. That means social media is a great opportunity for you to start building a digital footprint that reflects well on you.

Young men applied online for jobs at a job fair.

Social media can be useful in school too. You can learn about almost any topic or academic subject through social media. YouTube can be a good resource for educational videos on just about everything—changing a bike tire, solving a trigonometry problem, or even talking about an important issue with someone who disagrees with you. You can also use group chats or other methods to form study groups with your friends.

The social skills you learn by networking online will help you all your life. Learning to be polite, asking questions, working together, and using your curiosity to learn and build relationships will help you succeed in college, real-life relationships, and your career.

Digital skills themselves are also important. As you learn to manage accounts, apps, and platforms, as well as manipulate and troubleshoot hardware, you're mastering skills that more and more jobs will require. In the future,

Many popular apps are geared toward connecting people, whether socially or professionally.

you'll have opportunities for jobs that don't even exist today. But aptitude and confidence with digital platforms such as social media are sure to be key parts of those jobs.

Identity, Empathy, and Inclusion

Psychologists say that social media helps teens develop their unique identity. Before you present yourself to the world on social media, you think about what you believe, think, and prefer. This kind of self-awareness improves mental health. One survey of college freshmen showed that teens who expressed opinions on social media had a greater sense of well-being. Teens who communicated more online had greater self-concept clarity, or a better understanding of who they were.

In spite of growing concern about social networking—including worries about depression, isolation, addiction, and online safety—most teens report having a mostly positive relationship with social media. According to a 2018 survey by Pew Research Center, 81 percent of teens said it helps them feel more connected to friends. And 68 percent said it helps them feel as if they have people who will "support them through tough times."

Positive aspects of social media use for teens include feeling connected and supported.

However, the news isn't all positive. The survey did show some concerning numbers, with about 25 percent of teens saying that social media led to them feeling excluded and 26 percent saying it made them feel insecure. On the other hand, 71 percent said social media helped them feel *included,* and 69 percent said it helped them feel confident.

Many young people use social media to expand their experience of the world in a positive way. About two-thirds of teens in the survey said social media helps them "interact with individuals from diverse backgrounds, find different points of view, or show their support for causes or issues." Being online also helps many young people keep their friendships strong. About 60 percent said they spend time interacting with friends online every day or nearly every day.

While some concern is valid, it is clear that social media can be a positive influence in the lives of young people. The key to keeping it positive is to use it wisely and constructively.

Most Popular Online Groups Among Teenagers

The Pew Research Center analyzed a survey of 743 U.S. teens about their social media use, including the types of groups teens tend to be a part of online. Here are the percentages of teens who said they interact with groups and the focus of these groups:

(% of teens who spend time in online group)

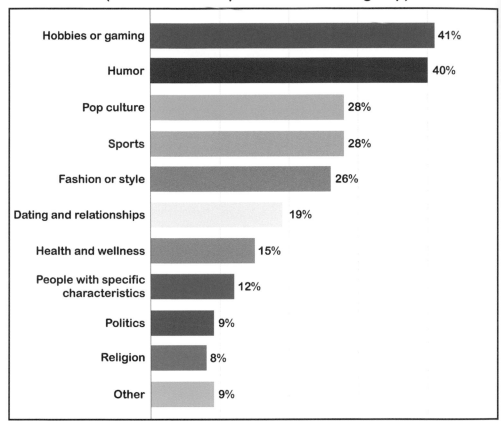

credit: https://www.pewresearch.org/internet/2018/11/28/teens-friendships-and-online-groups/#fnref-21833-2

CHAPTER 4

HERE COME THE TROLLS

Along with the benefits that we get from social media are a few negative aspects. One of the most difficult parts of life online is dealing with internet trolls.

In fairy tales, trolls are evil creatures who hide in the dark under bridges and attack people when they try

Internet trolls share some personality traits with fairy-tale trolls.

to cross. Similarly, internet trolls also hide in darkness— by being anonymous on the web. Internet trolls harass, embarrass, threaten, or otherwise hurt people online with whom they disagree—generally without revealing their identity.

One of the most common places where people troll is in the comments located after an online article or video. You may have heard the advice, "Never read the comments." That's because they often tend to get ugly, especially when the original content posters put themselves out there in a way that makes them vulnerable, such as posting a video they made on YouTube. Commenters might criticize someone's looks, race, gender, or performance in especially unkind ways. Trolls have even mocked recently deceased people on their memorial pages on Facebook. Hiding behind a username that isn't linked to their real identity makes it easier to be cruel.

FACT

The term *troll* originally came from the sport of fishing. In fishing, trolling means to draw a baited hook through the water in hopes of catching something. Internet trolls post their opinions online in the hope of upsetting someone or baiting them into an argument.

Online Cruelty

It's not just the comments at the bottom of videos, news stories, and social media posts. Interactions on Twitter, Facebook, Instagram, Snapchat, and most any other platform are ripe for nastiness. And much of the time, the websites do a poor job of regulating hate speech and bullying.

Sometimes the trolling stops at insults, but it frequently rises to harassment and threats. In especially bad cases, people are doxed. The term *dox* originally came from the phrase *dropping docs*, or finding someone's private documents and making them public. This happens when trolls find and post the victims' personal information, such as their social security numbers, bank account numbers, addresses, family member names, and more.

And then there's swatting—reporting a fake crime at someone's home or business to the police so that a Special Weapons and Tactics (SWAT) team breaks in. If authorities believe a dangerous crime is taking place in the building, they'll come in with guns drawn and ready to attack. Swatting has resulted in innocent victims being shot and killed by police.

Online pranks involving SWAT teams are dangerous and costly.

Women and members of ethnic minority groups tend to get the worst treatment online. Their bullying frequently includes death threats and threats of sexual violence. One high-profile example happened in 2012, when the feminist media critic and speaker Anita Sarkeesian started a Kickstarter campaign. She planned to fund a series of YouTube videos opposing video games with misogynistic content. When her campaign was successful and she began making the videos, she was viciously bullied on social media by male, anti-feminist gamers. She received bomb threats at speaking engagements, doxing threats, and rape threats. Someone even created a video game called *Beat Up Anita Sarkeesian.*

Anita Sarkeesian

Another feminist writer quit social media altogether after receiving threats of violence against her five-year-old daughter. In the United Kingdom, female Members of Parliament (MPs) received heavy abuse on Twitter leading up to the 2017 UK general election. Black female MP Diane Abbott received nearly half of those abusive tweets. Even taking Abbott out of the totals, black and Asian female MPs received about 35 percent more abusive tweets than white female MPs.

Who Are the Trolls?

So who are these trolls? The answer is anyone. Trolls come from all walks of life.

Jessica Moreno, who worked as the head of community at the social media platform Reddit, said that many people's idea of a socially isolated internet troll living in a basement while munching chips and gulping soda isn't accurate. Moreno saw firsthand the trolling behavior of Reddit users. "They would be a doctor, a lawyer, an inspirational speaker, a kindergarten teacher. They'd . . . be a

An online troll could be anyone.

normal person." Trolls are regular people who any of us might know in real life.

Scientists point out that humans have evolved to be kind to one another and to cooperate. That's how we have always survived. Being good to people didn't only help us with basic things such as finding food and protecting ourselves from the weather and predators. It also made things easier when interacting with others. Humans historically lived in small communities where we dealt with one another face-to-face all the time.

"In the small-scale societies that our ancestors were living in, all our interactions were with people that you were going to see again and interact with in the immediate future," said Professor David Rand, who directs the Human Cooperation Lab at Yale University in Connecticut. The lab's purpose is to help researchers understand how and why we cooperate. Humans have always been basically civil to one another, he said, because nobody wanted to be mean or take advantage of others who they'd have to see every day. It was just easier to be nice.

But what happens when people don't have to interact face-to-face? Some take advantage of online anonymity and insult or abuse others from the shadows.

Researchers at U.S. universities Stanford and Cornell conducted a study to understand why people troll. The answer comes down to two factors—a person's mood and the tone of other comments. The researchers required people to take a test. Some were given a very hard test while others were given a relatively easy one. The researchers assumed that the people who took the hard test would be in a worse mood afterward. Once they completed the test, the subjects were asked to read an article and post a comment. The article already had three comments. For some subjects, the comments were neutral in tone. For others, the comments were from trolls.

Feelings of anger, frustration, and helplessness lead some people to post cruel things online.

Among people who had either taken the tough test or read the troll's comments, about half posted mean, trolling comments of their own. The number rose to 68 percent for people who'd taken the difficult test *and* read the trolls' comments. Of the people who took the easy test and viewed neutral comments, only 35 percent posted trolling comments.

A Spiral of Negativity

These findings were backed up by a study of millions of posts on the CNN website. Researchers found that trolling comments were most often posted late at night and early in the week. Previous research had shown that those times are when people are most likely to be in bad moods. The study also found that people were more likely to comment negatively if one of their previous comments was recently flagged as inappropriate or if they'd participated in another discussion that included flagged comments.

"It's a spiral of negativity," said Jure Leskovec, a computer science professor at Stanford University in California and the senior author of the study. "Just one person waking up cranky can create a spark and, because of discussion context and voting, these sparks can spiral into cascades of bad behavior. Bad conversations lead to bad conversations."

Trolls tend to be people who have difficulty respecting different perspectives. This lack of respect can lead to justifying behavior that demeans and degrades others who don't agree with the troll. Trolling has particularly become a tool for the alt-right, a political movement that advocates for men's rights over women's rights, fights against immigration, and supports other ultra-conservative causes. However, people on the far left of the political spectrum who hold extremely liberal views can also be trolls. Other common social media trolls include hate groups such as white nationalists and incels, who are "involuntarily celibate" men angry with women for rejecting them.

FACT
President Donald Trump once doxed Senator Lindsey Graham, who at the time was a political opponent in the Republican primary race, by posting his phone number.

Donald J. Trump ✓
@realDonaldTrump
45th President of the United States of America

TWEETS
34.7K

Tweets

A Silencing Effect

For many, the risk of harassment online isn't worth the benefits. These people prefer to stay off social media or instead use it passively, rarely making their own posts. The result is fewer diverse voices online. It also makes social media a lot less fun.

Unfortunately, trolls don't seem to be going away. A 2017 Pew Research Center survey found that about 40 percent of American adults had experienced online abuse. Almost half of those received severe harassment such as physical threats and stalking. Of the women surveyed, 70 percent described online harassment as a "major problem."

RUSSIAN TROLLS AND THE 2016 PRESIDENTIAL ELECTION

Did Russians use social media to influence the 2016 U.S. presidential election? A study by the U.S. government found that they did.

According to the study, Russia's Internet Research Agency created fake social media accounts and spread false news and opinion stories. The agency's goal was to swing the U.S. vote in favor of Donald Trump. To do this, its employees created fake accounts, groups, and ads on Facebook, Twitter, and other platforms. Some of the accounts repeated false stories about Donald Trump's opponent, Hillary Clinton. Others referred to made-up news stories about fake events.

One example of a fake story was the Columbian Chemicals Plant explosion hoax. In September 2014, Russian researchers created a story about a completely fake explosion at a chemical plant in Centerville, Louisiana. Then they created fake versions of websites pretending to be local TV stations and newspapers. The fake websites showed fake footage of an explosion, and the social media accounts referred to the websites as evidence of the explosion. Trolls said the terrorist organization ISIS had claimed responsibility for the attack and said that President Barack Obama, who was a political ally of Hillary Clinton, wasn't doing enough to keep Americans safe.

Nearly 126 million Americans were reached by the Russians' fake Facebook accounts. In many cases, politicians and journalists believed some of the made-up accounts to be those of real people. Fake accounts even inspired rallies in U.S. cities such as Philadelphia and Miami.

Even though the U.S. government discovered the false social media accounts, they haven't stopped. U.S. researchers have evidence that the Russians are still using fake social media accounts to influence the outcome of future elections.

CHAPTER 5

SOCIAL OR ANTISOCIAL?

Not everyone is harassed or bullied by trolls online, but other negative influences of social media can be more common. And these downsides can have a powerful effect.

Humans need face-to-face socialization, especially when they're young and learning how to get along with others. When kids and teens hang out together in person, they gain important social skills. They learn to read facial expressions, body language, and even changes in vocal reactions. They engage in all sorts of tiny, real-time interactions that serve as experiments. *How do people react if I raise my voice this much? What happens if I smile while I say that? What if I make this face?* You don't necessarily think about these as experiments, but you're learning to react to social cues. When communicating through a screen, most of those social cues disappear, and your ability to develop social skills decreases.

Addiction and Anxiety

Scientists have found that social media can be addictive. That's because likes, shares, and positive comments act like a reward that releases dopamine in the brain. Dopamine is a neurochemical that gives you a sense of pleasure. It's the same chemical released when people do other addictive behaviors, such as smoke cigarettes or drink alcohol. So those likes and shares are literally rewarding your brain the same way other addictive behaviors do. This can set up a pattern where you need more and more likes to feel satisfied. Addictive pleasure from social media can lead to ignoring real-world enjoyment, such as face-to-face relationships.

Part of what makes social media so addictive is that it follows us everywhere. Platforms such as Facebook and

In-person communication helps develop life skills you can't learn online.

Instagram always exist, and we're always aware of them. Even if you're not updating your status or checking social media, you likely can still be reached by text message. As a result, users feel highly connected to one another. Even though connection is good, everyone also needs time to be alone, relax, and regroup.

With all that connection going on, it might seem odd that many teens and adults feel lonely. But it's a common result. If you don't get a reply to your message or likes for your post, it's natural to feel sad or unliked.

The constant pursuit of "likes" can cause stress and anxiety.

FACT

Surveys have shown that teens who spend more time online report more mental health issues. However, some research shows that it may not be that social media is causing these issues. Instead it may be the other way around—when teens are depressed, they use social media more.

Add to that the burden of comparing yourself to everyone else. Everyone puts their best self online—their most flattering pictures, wittiest thoughts, and biggest accomplishments. Of course we all know this, but we still can't help comparing ourselves to everyone else's best self that we see online. Image and peer acceptance are important, especially for teens. The number of likes you get can feel very personal—similar to votes for or against you as a person.

As a result, many teens spend a great deal of time on their online images and brand. And it makes sense. If you can make yourself look cooler, why wouldn't you? Girls in particular spend a lot of time taking selfies, editing them, and adding filters. Girls have long had to compare themselves to airbrushed models who look unrealistically beautiful. But now their peers have the same ability to alter images. This creates more pressure on girls to perfect their own images in order to compete. But all that editing and comparing can lead to anxiety, insecurity, and lower self-esteem.

FACT

A poll of plastic surgeons found that 42 percent of them have been asked to perform procedures for improved selfies and pictures on social media platforms.

SELFIE GENERATION

Teens born after 2000 are the first generation to have grown up with social media. This means they've lived with the benefits and the drawbacks of an online life. One drawback scientists worry about is the impact of a "selfie culture." A 2015 poll found that women between 16 and 25 years old spend more than five hours a week taking selfies. They take an average of seven pictures to get the right one.

There's nothing specifically wrong with selfies. They can be silly or just for fun. But they can also become a way of measuring a person's self-worth. Too much comparing yourself to others is a recipe for lowering your self-esteem. One study found that for girls, more time spent looking at photos on Facebook led to higher dissatisfaction with their weight. It also contributes to self-objectification, or viewing yourself as an object valued only for your appearance.

Liking the way you look is an important part of your self-esteem. But for deeper long-term happiness, we need many sources of self-esteem. You can get that through team sports, academics, creative or performing arts, and other personal accomplishments.

Cyberbullying

Our friends, followers, and other online connections can sometimes be cruel—often by accident or carelessness. For example, friends may ignore a message from you, or they may post about something fun they're doing without you. It's easy to be misunderstood or hurtful without the benefit of seeing someone's facial expressions. All of this is just another aspect of the pressure cooker that social media can be. But social media friends also sometimes hurt one another intentionally.

The same anonymity that makes it easy and tempting for people to troll also contributes to the temptation to harass or cyberbully others. Even if you know who the person is, the separation of being online makes it easier to be mean. When you are talking to someone face-to-face, you can see how they react to your words. If you see someone feeling pain that you've caused, it becomes harder to say mean things. But social media hides those reactions.

People might make fun of you or insult you. They might spread rumors about you or post an embarrassing photo or video of you. With social media there's a built-in audience, which ramps up these cruel acts and can make them feel especially painful.

A 2018 Pew Research Center survey of teens found that about 45 percent said they feel overwhelmed by "drama" on social media, with 13 percent reporting that they feel this way "a lot." In a separate Pew survey of teens, 59 percent said they have experienced cyberbullying. The numbers were similar for both boys and girls, but girls were more likely to report being the targets of online rumor-spreading or nonconsensual explicit messages. According to the survey, 90 percent of teens believe that online harassment is a problem.

Problems IRL

On top of the issues with harassment and mental health, social media can also have negative impacts on our offline interactions. Have you ever tried to talk with someone while they're scrolling through Instagram? Even if they're not totally ignoring you, they certainly aren't giving you their full attention. And adults are as guilty as kids. Moms check Facebook at the dinner table. Dads miss their kids' soccer goals because they have their eyes glued to their phones. These behaviors have negative effects on relationships. Family members need to be available to one another, which means talking together and showing each other our faces—not the tops of our heads.

Many times, social media rudeness seeps into our offline interactions. On social media, we're conditioned to post our opinions. The whole idea of social media is that our opinions are important and worthy of being broadcast to the world. But often, the best way to get an online reaction to our opinions is to deliver them rudely. Over time, we may begin to adopt that attitude in face-to-face encounters as well.

Social media has many direct links to poor physical health. The blue light the devices emit stimulates neurons in the brain and reduces the ability to produce melatonin, a hormone that leads to sleep. Just having your phone near your bed is telling your body that it's time to be awake. Even when they do fall asleep, many teens check social media if they happen to wake up during the night.

Too much time online comes at a direct cost of time spent doing physical things. If you're snapping selfies, posting, commenting, and liking, you aren't exercising or interacting in the world. We all need good sleep and plenty of exercise to live healthy lives.

FACT

Social media may help teens develop healthy lifestyles. Seeing peers exercising, eating healthy food, or being creative can encourage other users to do the same.

If you're one of the many teens who checks social media while doing other tasks such as homework, you're interfering with your learning and undercutting your performance. Switching constantly between two or more tasks, such as checking Snapchat and reading a story for English class, results in poorer concentration on both tasks. That means homework will likely take you longer—and who wants that?

Healthy Social Media Use

We can still enjoy the benefits of social media. But to keep your relationship with social media healthy, it helps to have a plan. Be mindful and deliberate about when, how, and especially why you're using it. You might create rules for how long you'll use social media and at what times. Some people give themselves time limits, such as one hour each day. Good starter guidelines are to never use your phone during meals or within an hour of going to bed.

Think about why you're logging on and what you want to see. Understand why you have the urge to check your social media accounts. If it's just because you're bored, you can turn off notifications so you're not constantly tempted to check them.

"Before you pick up your device, understand why you're picking it up," said Dr. Alexandra Hamlet, a clinical psychologist at the Child Mind Institute in New York City. "What emotional state are you in? Are you anxious? Picking up that phone to check to see what's on social media is probably going to heighten that anxiety. The same with sadness. It's just going to make it worse."

FACT

If you ever feel depressed or feel like hurting yourself, please get help right away. Talk to an adult you trust or contact a help line such as the National Suicide Prevention Lifeline: 1-800-273-8255 or https://suicidepreventionlifeline.org.

Perhaps most important of all, be kind. Don't bully or pressure others, and think twice before posting something that affects others. Ask yourself: *Is this true? Is it fair? Even if it is, could it make anyone feel bad?* Don't take photos or videos of others without their consent. And don't like or share mean posts. You can even speak up when you see mean behavior online among friends. If you have a problem with something posted online, send the poster a private message with your concerns instead of posting it on their page for all to see. Or even better, talk to them about it in person.

We can thrive with social media if we control our use of it, not the other way around. When you are with others, be present. That means don't check your phone while you're talking with people. And make sure you're finding time to be active IRL. That's where life is happening.

Smartphones and Mental Health

Smartphones came out in 2007. By 2015, nearly 75 percent of teens owned or had access to one. A 2017 research paper published in the journal *Clinical Psychological Science* found that between 2010 and 2015, depression rates rose among teens by 33 percent, among females more so than males. Of course, much more research is needed to prove whether or not smartphone and social media use causes or contributes to teenage depression.

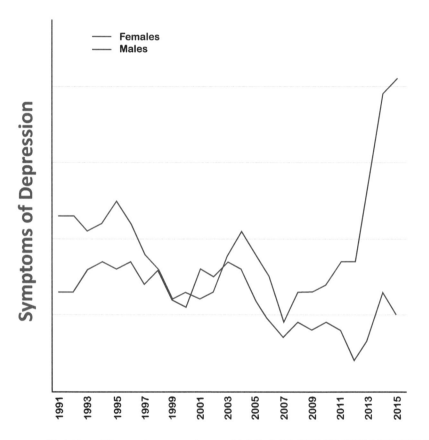

credit: https://journals.sagepub.com/doi/full/10.1177/2167702617723376

Get Involved

If you're dealing with bullying or trolls on social media, experts advise you to stay calm. Block or ignore people who are harassing you or tell them to stop if you feel confident doing so. However, don't retaliate. Tell someone, such as family or trusted friends, and ask them to help you. Take screenshots and report online harassment to the social media service where it's happening. If you are being threatened, report it to the police.

Is social media affecting your emotional well-being? Be honest with yourself about your relationship with social media. Ask yourself:

- What is my purpose in using social media? Does my online behavior reflect my purpose?

- Does social media cause me anxiety?

- Do I sometimes log in for a quick look, only to end up spending much longer than I intended?

- Do I have difficulty taking a break from social media for a day? A week? A month? If so, what makes these breaks difficult for me?

- Have I been harassed on social media? Have I harassed others?

Most people don't have to give up social media in order to lead a healthy life. Balance is key. Be active offline. Find ways to feel good about yourself that aren't tied to social media. Play sports, get exercise, participate in clubs, be creative in some way, or spend time with your friends in person. You can listen to music, go on a walk or bike ride, or just hang out—but not on your phones.

Here are some other tips:

- Together with your family, make technology-free zones, such as the dining room and the bedrooms.

- You can also make technology-free times, such as mealtime and at least one hour before bedtime.

- When you talk with people, give them your full attention.

- Unfollow accounts that are negative, unhealthy, or make you feel bad.

- Track your screen time and make a conscious effort to reduce it.

- Use a computer for social media instead of a cell phone.

- Turn off notifications so you aren't constantly checking for any updates.

- Set your device's screen to grayscale so you aren't as distracted by bright colors and photos on the screen.

Most importantly, you can use social media for good. Promote positive accounts or create a positive social media campaign of your own. You can develop a campaign about eating healthy, combating bullying, helping people in need, or any other positive ideas you may have.

Glossary

alt-right—a far-right political movement that advocates for men's rights over women's rights, fights against immigration, and supports other ultra-conservative causes

blog—a website or part of a website where a writer regularly posts personal reflections and ideas on a particular topic; short for weblog

cyberbullying—bullying that takes place online

data—factual information

digital footprint—the trail of data you create while using the internet, which includes the websites you visit, emails you send, and information you submit to online services

dox—a way of harassing someone online by finding and posting their personal information such as social security number, bank account numbers, address, and family member names

hashtag—a word or phrase preceded by the symbol # that classifies or categorizes the accompanying text, such as a tweet

misogyny—contempt for and prejudice against women

neurochemical—a drug or other substance that affects the nervous system

platform—the environment in which a piece of computer software operates

protocol—a set of rules governing the exchange or transmission of data between computer devices

social skills—tools that people use to communicate, get along with others, make friends, develop healthy relationships, learn, ask for help, get their needs met, protect themselves, and interact with others in a positive way

swat—to report a fake crime to someone's home so that a SWAT team breaks in

tweet—a 240-character message sent on the social media platform Twitter

Additional Resources

Critical Thinking Questions

1. Could you give up social media for one full day? How about for a week or longer? What do you think your answers say about your relationship with social media?

2. Have you ever acted mean toward someone on social media? If so, why did you do it? How did you feel afterward? What could you do to make it up to the person?

3. What are some ways you can spread positivity online?

Further Reading

Bocci, Goali Saedi. *The Social Media Workbook for Teens: Skills to Help You Balance Screen Time, Manage Stress & Take Charge of Your Life.* Oakland, CA: Instant Help Books, 2019.

Hinman, Bonnie. *Teens and Social Media.* San Diego: ReferencePoint Press, 2019.

Lanier, Jaron. *Ten Arguments for Deleting Your Social Media Accounts Right Now.* New York: Henry Holt, 2018.

The New York Times Editorial Staff. *Cyberbullying: A Deadly Trend.* New York: New York Times Educational Publishing, 2019.

Internet Sites

MindWise: How to Have a Healthy Relationship with Social Media
https://www.mindwise.org/blog/mental-health/how-to-have-a-healthy-relationship-with-social-media/

TeensHealth: Online Safety
https://kidshealth.org/en/teens/internet-safety.html?ref=search

Source Notes

p. 6, "We do want to thank..." N'dea Yancey-Bragg, "Missing girl Salem Sabatka found safe after 'heroes' lead Texas police to her kidnapper," *USA Today*, May 19, 2019, https://www.usatoday.com/story/news/nation/2019/05/19/8-year-old-found-safe-heroes-tip-texas-police/3732770002

p. 8, "Going to Africa..." Jon Ronson. *So You've Been Publicly Shamed*. New York: Riverhead Books, 2015.

p. 8, "Only an insane person..." Ibid., p. 72.

p. 9, "...with social media, we've..." Ibid., p. 78.

p. 30, "I'll never forget the boys..." Ark's Foundation, Nd., http://www.arksfoundation.org/about-us.html

p. 30, "Regarding our message, we..." Smart Social, "7 Teens Using Social Media for Good Deeds," October 16, 2019, https://smartsocial.com/teens-using-social-media-good-deeds

p. 35, "interact with individuals from..." Monica Anderson and Jingjing Jiang, Pew Survey, "Teens' Social Media Habits and Experiences," Pew Research Center, November 28, 2018, https://www.pewinternet.org/2018/11/28/teens-social-media-habits-and-experiences/

p. 41, "They would be a doctor..." Joel Stein, "How Trolls Are Ruining the Internet," *Time*, August 18, 2016, https://time.com/4457110/internet-trolls/

p. 41, "In the small-scale societies..." Gaia Vince, "Evolution explains why we act differently online," BBC Future, April 3, 2018, https://www.bbc.com/future/article/20180403-why-do-people-become-trolls-online-and-in-social-media

p. 43, "It's a spiral of negativity..." Rachel Hosie, "Online trolls: Why do people become cyberbullies?" *Independent*, March 7, 2017, https://www.independent.co.uk/life-style/online-trolls-why-people-become-cyber-bullies-social-media-twitter-facebook-study-cornell-stanford-a7616126.html

p. 54, "Before you pick up your device..." Caroline Miller, "Does Social Media Cause Depression?" Child Mind Institute, https://childmind.org/article/is-social-media-use-causing-depression/

All sites accessed April 23, 2020.

Select Bibliography

Books

Ronson, Jon. *So You've Been Publicly Shamed.* New York: Riverhead Books, 2015.

Steiner-Adair, Catherine and Teresa H. Barker. *The Big Disconnect: Protecting Childhood and Family Relationships in the Digital Age.* New York: HarperCollins Publishers Inc., 2013.

Websites and Articles

Anderson, Monica, "A Majority of Teens Have Experienced Some Form of Cyberbullying," Pew Research Center, September 27, 2018, https://www.pewresearch.org/internet/2018/09/27/a-majority-of-teens-have-experienced-some-form-of-cyberbullying/

Anderson, Monica and Jingjing Jiang, "Teens' Social Media Habits and Experiences," Pew Research Center, November 28, 2018, https://www.pewinternet.org/2018/11/28/teens-social-media-habits-and-experiences/

Ark's Foundation, http://www.arksfoundation.org/home.html

Ehmke, Rachel, "How Using Social Media Affects Teenagers," Child Mind Institute, https://childmind.org/article/how-using-social-media-affects-teenagers/

Ehmke, Rachel, "What Selfies Are Doing to Self-Esteem," Child Mind Institute, https://childmind.org/article/what-selfies-are-doing-to-girls-self-esteem/

Hosie, Rachel, "Online Trolls: Why Do People Become Cyberbullies?" *Independent*, March 7, 2017, https://www.independent.co.uk/life-style/online-trolls-why-people-become-cyber-bullies-social-media-twitter-facebook-study-cornell-stanford-a7616126.html

Miller, Caroline, "Does Social Media Cause Depression?" Child Mind Institute, https://childmind.org/article/is-social-media-use-causing-depression/

Smart Social, "7 Teens Using Social Media for Good Deeds," October 16, 2019, https://smartsocial.com/teens-using-social-media-good-deeds

Stein, Joel, "How Trolls Are Ruining the Internet," *Time*, August 18, 2016, https://time.com/4457110/internet-trolls/

Vince, Gaia, "Evolution Explains Why We Act Differently Online," BBC Future, April 3, 2018, https://www.bbc.com/future/article/20180403-why-do-people-become-trolls-online-and-in-social-media

Yancey-Bragg, N'dea, "Missing girl Salem Sabatka found safe after 'heroes' lead Texas police to her kidnapper," *USA Today*, May 19, 2019, https://www.usatoday.com/story/news/nation/2019/05/19/8-year-old-found-safe-heroes-tip-texas-police/3732770002

All sites accessed April 23, 2020.

About the Author

Eric Braun is the author of books for readers of all ages on topics such as sports, history, current issues, and biographies. He is also a children's book editor and a McKnight Artist Fellow for his fiction. He lives in Minneapolis with his wife, sons, and dog, Willis the Scaredycat.

Index